W9-BBH-137

A FIESTA OF TOUGH CHOICES

Contemporary
Art in the Wake of
Cultural Policies

ISBN: 978-82-997365-3-4
Printed by Wassberg + Skotte Tryckeri, Stockholm, 2007
Published and distributed by Torpedo Press

CONTENTS

PREFACE

Multiculturalism is a little too easy to dismiss. In political terms for the Right, it poses a threat to traditions and national identity. For the Left, it often means food festivals, post-Marxist culturalism, or reactionary community spokesmen. As with discussions of globalization, perhaps the crux of the problem lies in the tools at our disposal. The critical terminology is awkward or embarrassing at best, dangerous at worst. At the very least, a more exact language might help define the terms of engagement more precisely. Following the Swedish government's declaration of *2006: Year of Cultural Diversity* (in Swedish "Mångkulturåret"), we looked to artists and theorists with a capacity for reassessing standard cultural terminologies and revisiting their critical potential. In other words, we took quite literally, the government decree that all State institutions launch a multicultural project for 2006. But in doing so, we tried to engage critically with notions of diversity in and of themselves. We also attempted to trace the typical aesthetic and formal trappings of a public discussion of this kind. One example of a vital critical discourse in this context is Postcolonial Theory. Emerging in the 1980's amongst other things such thought analyzed the complicity of Western intellectual traditions in various forms of colonialism, old and new. According to its harshest critics, because of its rapid institutionalization Post Colonialism spawned a newer, updated version of the same colonialism. In the light of this, what are the dangers of academic engagement, and other top-down gestures of goodwill?

A Fiesta of Tough Choices eventually became a festival-inspired exhibition with two seminars that took place at Iaspis, March 2006. This publication not only documents the event but takes the discussions that arose there one step further.

We very much hope you enjoy the book.

Maria Lind
Tirdad Zolghadr

SOUNDTRACK FOR
A FIESTA OF TOUGH CHOICES (2006)
1 MIN LOOP

Peter Geschwind

A small boy goes wild on a percussion and keyboard. The material is edited in Final Cut Pro following a techno-loop pattern in the programme Garageband. Special thanks to Leo Loveless/percussion and keyboard.

MULTICULTURALISM
AND THE FAREWELL STATE—
THE CASE OF SWEDEN

Edda Manga

Discourses of multicultural-
ism, pluralism and cultural diversity are often portrayed as
the opposite to racism and ethno-nationalism. However,
ideas that are central to these discourses, such as "respect for
other cultures" and the "right to develop one's cultural heri-
tage", are formulated in similar terms as the colonialist ideal of
"separate development", and multicultural celebrations are
often organized as mini World Exhibitions where different
nationalities are represented by typical cultural expressions,
distinct products, and specific knowledge.[1]

Meanwhile, ethnic identity has been given a predomi-
nant place in the rhetoric of both the traditional and the
new xenophobic political parties in Europe, where multi-
culturality is seen as one of the challenges of globalization
to the political model of the welfare-state. In this context,
multiculturalism is seen as a problem to democracy and the
welfare-state because it erodes the common values that are
supposedly central to them.[2]

The development of nation-states in Europe runs parallel
to the history of colonial expansion and its multiple discourses
on racial and cultural difference. Nation-states used to connect
citizenship to racial categories, and state policies concerned
with the production of a national population (folk) included

methods directly aimed at improving the racial stock.[3] In Sweden, the construction of the national welfare-state was formulated in terms of a "good home" for the Swedish folk by its "founding father" Per Albin Hansson. Per Albin envisioned the Swedish model as a place with a family-like sense of community, a "folk home" for all citizens.[4] In the ideal home, there are no privileged children and no neglected ones, Per Albin explained. Nobody tries to obtain gains to the detriment of other family members because the economy of a good family is common. The good home is a space of equality, devotion and cooperation.

The qualifier "folk" represented a worthy effort to wrest the conception of the Swedish nation from the bourgeoisie, to the benefit of the notion of a good home, but it proved problematic. During the decades to follow, the equality of the Swedish people merged with the notion of the Swedish people as a homogeneous, *genetic community*.[5] State-policies aimed at making good citizens of the population were formulated in accordance with eugenic principles including positive measures like education programs, health care and public housing, as well as negative ones taken by state run sterilization programs, to prevent the reproduction of "less fit" or "abnormal" Swedes (mentally ill, or unmarried yet sexually active women) and of groups perceived as racially/culturally different (saamis, gypsies, "tattare").

As the critique of racism gained international recognition following the Second World War, and "race" was replaced by "ethnicity" and "culture" as a way of conceiving difference, the question of "abnormality" and "difference" in the welfare-state came to be reformulated in terms of "assimilation". In a period when former colonial centers started receiving waves of immigrants from former colonies and poorer regions, the dominant culture of the "host country" was represented as universal, whereas cultural difference was ascribed to newcomers.[6] Assimilation was thus conceived as a form of culturally neutral modernization.

During the years of post-war economical boom, when offices of labor recruitment in Southern Europe tried to attract immigrants to Sweden, assimilation was the privileged model.[7] Cultural differences were represented as temporal and immigration policies aimed at making Swedes of the newcomers. When the boom period faded in the early 1970's, however, Sweden banned labor immigration from all non-Nordic countries and the question of repatriation of guest workers already in the country was widely discussed.

A 1974 report on the "special problems that immigrants face in Sweden" marks a shift from an assimilationist approach toward an "integrationist" one.[8] The report stated that the Swedish policy toward immigrants should be oriented by principles of equality, freedom of choice and cooperation, meaning that equality didn't presuppose that the immigrants adopted Swedish culture, and that they should be free to uphold their own if they so wished. In the latter case, "respecting" the immigrants' culture was to facilitate future repatriation. Henceforth, the Swedish population was conceived of as a culturally homogeneous majority and a category of culturally diverse minorities.

Following the 1972 ban of labor migration, immigration was restricted to the categories of "political refugees" and "family reunion". The former became a backbone of the 1970's rhetoric of Swedish immigration policy as one of generosity and solidarity, and played an important part in Sweden's self-identity as avant-garde. Sweden was represented as anti-racist, clean from any colonial past and engaged in the development of the Third World. The Leftist wave of the time, with its engagement against the u.s. war in Vietnam and support for the anti-colonial liberation movements in Africa, contributed to a representation of the Immigrant as a radical political refugee (an African American deserter, a Greek or Latin American socialist) from an unjust regime, nourishing the image of Sweden as a democratic oasis in a troubled world.

This image was challenged in the early 1980's as the flow of political refugees shifted to include citizens of Iran, Iraq, Somalia, coinciding with the ideological shift to the Right, intiated in the west during the regimes of Thatcher and Reagan. Many of the new refugees were Muslims, perceived as racially different, escaping from conflicts seemingly harder to identify with. Mainstream political discourse began to adopt market fundamentalist tenets and immigration was seen as an economic burden, and an example of unsound public expenditure.

As the 1980's gave way to the 1990's, the Generosity Model was definitively shattered. In the 1991 election, right wing politicians – noticeably from the new Populist Party, *Ny Demokrati*, which made an unprecedented rapid entry into parliament on the basis of an anti-immigration political program – directed their attack on Social Democratic immigration policies. Sweden had taken care of too many immigrants, which was costly for the state budget and created "cultural problems".[9] Although there was a consensus to reject the policies of *Ny Demokrati* among the established parties, their rhetorical and electoral success effectively changed the range of the discussion. Ethnic difference became an explanation for social problems replacing the former privileged socio-economic categories. Although *Ny Demokrati* imploded and disappeared from the landscape with the next election, their arguments had been introduced in the programs of established parties.[10]

During the 1990's, the perception of ethnic difference as a political problem became normalized and appropriated also by the Social Democratic regime as it was reelected in 1994. "Integration" and "illegal immigration" where represented as important questions of national and European concern. Instead of the former pride for its "generosity", Swedish immigration-policy was depicted as outdated and un-European. Sweden closed its borders for Third World countries, preempting the application of Schengen regulations.

In 2006 a new perspective was introduced through a multilayered state report on structural discrimination. Departing from a critique of earlier conceptions of the "integration problem" as a question of the difficulties to integrate "others" this report focused on structural and institutional discrimination.[11] A number of processes that facilitate discrimination were observed in diverse areas, notably housing, health, education and representation in both media and political arenas. The most important were "othering" (categorizing part of the population as immigrants as opposed to "Swedes"), dominance (acquisition and reproduction of a hierarchical power relation by physical and symbolic violence) and control (monopolizing positions of authority so that other's access to essential goods and representation must go through "Swedes"). The report proposes a reformulation of the political task of integration toward a politics of social solidarity from a global perspective rather than from a limited national one. It concluded somewhat optimistically that the time when it was possible to think of social solidarity in terms of « ein Volk, ein Reich » was over.

Published during *2006: Year of Cultural Diversity* the report was aggressively rejected and its contributing case studies met with deafening silence. With the 2006 elections, Swedish mainstream politics leaped in the opposite direction. A right wing alliance was elected and two xenophobic parties, *Sverigedemokraterna* and *Nationaldemokraterna* made a notice-able impact on the national agenda. As with *Ny Demokrati*, the mainstream attitude to the ultra nationalist parties was seemingly paradoxical. While publicly condemned as politi-cal outcasts, their anti-immigration constituency was hardly ignored, and key elements of their agenda tended to influence mainstream party programs on questions of immigration and integration.

Both *Sverigedemokraterna* and *Nationaldemokraterna* op-pose what they call the "social experiment of multicultural-ism" on nationalist grounds. But their concept of nation-hood has adapted to the cultural turn of the new discourse of difference, leaving out race as the central category. Their argument can thus be recognized as "multicultural", but on a global rather than on a state-level. *Nationaldemokraterna* see themselves as ethno-pluralists that depart from the idea that every ethnic group must be acknowledged rights as if they were individuals. They want a world with a "multiplicity of ethnic groups". Instead of taking in a flow of immigrants with "foreign cultural values", Sweden should invest in local aid to underdeveloped countries so that they can sustain their population and develop their own homeland. But identification with western nations remains a priority. As *Sverigedemokraterna* state in the English version of their homepage: "Immigration, crime, globalization are all issues that affect every western country on the planet. We nationalists are all in the same boat, and should accordingly support one another as much as possible."

A number of elements (i. e. language tests before naturalization; expulsion of immigrants convicted for minor crimes; repayment of social securities granted during the asylum-seeking process) from the platforms of *Sverigedemokraterna* and *Nationaldemokraterna* were adopted by mainstream political parties – noticeably the "liberal" *Folkpartiet,* provoking the *Sverigedemokraterna* to publicly welcome *Folkpartiet* into its fold.[12]

What xenophobic groups, traditional parties and liberal multiculturalists have in common is the conception that it is possible and meaningful to see populations as mosaics of distinct, monolithic "cultures" that are constant over time. By attaching political measures to ethnicity, this conception sustains the (post)colonial production of exclusionary differences and privileges.[13] This politization of ethnicity and culture operates in the intersection between the nationalist discourse of the welfare-state and the global logic of opposition between "universal" values vs. "radical others".[14]

The celebration of multiculturalism – as exemplified by the festivities of the *Mångkulturåret* (2006: Year of Cultural Diversity) – paradoxically articulates this culturalist consensus while claiming to oppose its exclusionary consequences. Institutionalized multiculturalism operates as a difference-producing machine which, as it reaches out towards "culturally different" groups and marginalized actors, tends to generate interest groups committed to their own preservation.[15] Favoring a static conception of ethnic collectivities instead of dynamic power struggles and conjunctive alliances, multicultural political representation still asks: "take me to your leader". In the economic sphere multiculturalism is welcomed as "ethnic marketing", a form of capitalization of ethnic identity that at the same time studies and produces ethnically specific forms of consumption. Cultural diversity is thus inscribed in the world of enterprise as a resource in a colonial economy: it is imported raw, processed and resold for exotistic consumption in the metropolis and status consumption in the peripheries.

Does this mean that we are inevitably bound to reproduce the colonial order of things? Not necessarily. Instead of an ethnocracy, in which the political community is imagined to be based on birth into a nation, in which equality is thought of as brotherhood, and in which an ethnic homogeneity (folk) is represented by a parliament, we should aim at developing a democracy with the political community based on residence instead of birth, friendship instead of brotherhood, and participation instead of representation.[16] Hereby a celebration of diversity may reach beyond the current political usage of multiculturalism to become a vehicle for radical change.

Notes

1. On the colonialist discourse on separate development see Peter Fry, "Cultures of Difference: the aftermath of Portuguese and British colonial policies in Southern Africa", in *Social Anthropology* (v,8, n. 2, 2000), 117–144.

2. For an analysis of the discussion on nationalism, multicultural-ism and unity in Canada see Gerald Kemerman, *Multicullltural Nationalism: Civilizing Difference, Constituting Community* (Vancouver, 2005).

3. Gunnar Broberg and Mattias Tydén, (*Oönskade i folkhemmet: Rashygien och steriliseringar i Sverige*, Unwanted in the *folkhem*. Eugenics and sterilizations in Sweden), Stockholm, 1991.

4. *Per Albin om folkhemmet: Per Albin Hanssons tal om folkhemmet – medborgarhemmet i riksdagens remissdebatt* 1928, Sveriges socialdemokratiska arbetarparti, Stockholm, 1989.

5. On the idea of Sweden as a homogeneous genetic community see Maja Hagerman, *Det Rena Landet. Om konsten att uppfinna sina förfäder*, Stockholm, 2006. See also Christian Catomeris, *Det ohyggliga arvet: Sverige och främlingen genom tiderna*, Stockholm, 2004.

6. For an already classic analysis of this dynamic from a lacanian per-spective see Homi Bhabha, *The Location of Culture,* London: Routledge 1994.

7. See Saskia Sassen, *Guests and Aliens,* New York, 1999.

8. *Invandrarutredningen,* SOU (Statens offentliga utredningar) 1974:69 och 1974:70, Stockholm.

9. On the acceleration of racism and discrimination in Sweden during the 90's see Allan Pred, *Even in Sweden. Racisms, Racialized Spaces, and the Popular Geographical Imagination*, Berkeley: University of California Press 2000.

10. Kristina Boréus, *Diskrimineringens retorik: en studie av svenska val-rörelser* 1988–2002, SOU, Stockholm: Synposion, 2006) 52.

11. *Integrationens svarta bok. Agenda för jämnlikhet och social sammanhåll-ning. Slutbetänkande av utredningen om makt, integration och strukturell diskrimin-ering,* SOU, Stockholm, 2006), 79.

12. 'Jimmie Åkesson: 'Glädjande att de etablerade partierna anam-mar vår politik', in SD-*Kuriren* (05/05/31). 'Pressmeddelande: Folkpartiets

utspel är välkommet', in sd-*Kuriren* (05/03/02). 'Sverigedemokraterna
välkomnar Mauricio Rojas som medlem', in sd-*Kuriren* (06/01/25).

13. See MichaelAzar, *Den koloniala bumerangen: från Schibbolet till kör-kort i svenskhet,* Stockholm, 2006.

14. See Yegenoglu, Meyda, 'Liberal Multiculturalism and the Ethics of Hospitality in the Age of Globalization', in *Postmodern Culture,* (Vol. 13, no 2, Jan. 2003).

15. For an intimate critique of this problem see T. Minh-ha Thrinh *Woman, Native, Other,* (Bloomington: Indiana University Press, 1989).

16. See Rachel Buff, *Immigration and the Political Economy of Home* (Berkeley: University Press, 2000); Jacques Derrida, *The Politics of Friendship* (London: Verso, 1997) Ernesto Laclau and Chantal Mouffe, *Hegemony and Socialist Strategy. Towards a Radical Democratic Politics* (London: Verso, 1985). Saskia Sassen, 'The Repositioning of Citizenship. Emergent Subjects and Spaces for Politics', in *The New Centennial Review* (3.2, Michigan, 2003).

FERAL TRADE CATERING (2006)

Kate Rich

For the project *A Fiesta of Tough Choices, Feral Trade* was provided a catering stand, serving Third World refreshments (coffee from El Salvador; wild-grown mountain antidepressants from Bulgaria).

FERAL TRADE

Kate Rich

Feral Trade was set up as a sole-trader grocery business, in order to trade goods across social networks. This process was called Feral Trade to distinguish it from other methods like Fair Trade or Free Trade.

The first registered Feral Trade took place in 2003 – with the import of 30 KG of coffee direct from Codecano in San Pedro Nonualco, El Salvador, to the Cube Microplex in Bristol, UK – a transaction established via mutual acquaintances and conducted by email and SMS. Coffee from the same source is now distributed around the UK and Europe, avoiding the official channels of marketing and distribution in preference of individualised relations. Within an art context, this hand-freight network often uses other artists, curators and journalists as mules. On conclusion of each coffee shipment, the accumulated distribution data (buyers, cultural placements, media and reviews) are compiled and returned to San Pedro, for the scrutiny of the co-operative and its board. Other goods in current circulation include mountain-grown antidepressants from the Bulgaria-Greece periphery, and fresh sweets from Iran.

Feral Trade aims to offset the folklore of Fair Trade packaging – the dense foliage of happy farmers who use their profits for their children's education – by extending its attention to a range of other agents and relations active in a product's global transit.

Date: Tue, 11 Apr 2006 14:12:35 +0100 (BST)
From: kate rich
To: "Ricardo Andres Yglesias M."
Subject: report and new order

hi Ricardo

I hope you and the Co-op are well, and apologies that it's been a long time since
I've been in touch.

First, I wanted to send you a report on last shipment's coffee distribution -
I've sold most of the 200kg, with about 50-80 bags currently remaining.

New buyers include Bristol City Council's department of urban environmental
issues, the Better Food Company (an organic grocer in Bristol), and also distribution
through cultural organisations in Sweden, Luxembourg, Brussels,Edinburgh, Zurich,
London, as well as the Cube Microplex. As before,distribution is small-scale
(5-10 bags at a time) but the appreciation is substantial.

The coffee has appeared in an article in Bidoun Art Magazine , please
see http://www.bidoun.com/issues/issue_6/02_all.html#article and also
on the website of a gallery in Zurich, http://www.cabaretvoltaire.ch/aktuell/
aktuell.php?ID=32 and has been reviewed on a london cultural website, http:
//www.furtherfield.org/displayreview.php?From=Index&review_id=142%0D

Additionally, several packs of coffee have been delivered to Iran, and one to an
NGO in Afghanistan (my contact there used to work in El Salvador, many years
ago), plus several bags to the USA where I hope to establish a network of buyers
later in the year.

So overall, the project is going well.

Regarding a new shipment: I would hope to place an order soon if this is
convenient, for 200 kg. Division is 150 kg beans, and 50 kg ground coffee.

There was a problem with the last shipment that has slowed down sales, in that
the ground coffee was too coarse for European coffee-makers. This meant I have
had to re-grind the coffee here, which has caused some difficulty. Do you still have
the sample I sent as guide? I am hoping you could match this grind for the next
shipment.

I would also hope to pay the same price as previously, $8 per kilo for the coffee,
plus shipping costs, if this is agreeable to the co-operative.

I look forward to hear from you,
Regards,

Kate

THE SUBLIMATION OF POVERTY

Timothy Brennan

Much of what needs saying about poverty is resisted by intellectuals and artists because, although brutally true, it is no longer, in a market sense, 'interesting'. To say, 'capitalism thrives on inequality, and its major commodity is poverty' is like saying 'television makes you stupid'. Both statements are too obvious to be shocking or instructive. But then, strangely, by never being spoken openly they fall into another dimension, and it is in this way that the obvious becomes elusive.

The artist, who can never be anything but interesting, typically responds to crisis with archness, irony, and spectacle. In this way the boundaries are blurred between hatred for intolerable conditions of life and respect for the system's ability to punish, slander, or render irrelevant its dissidents. A shrewd indulgence in political masochism becomes the calling card of artistic maturity and depth. Balancing two sides, the artist implodes, learning to deploy an image of resistance that has been structurally adjusted to fit a transgressive – rather than anti-systemic – play on prevailing aesthetic tastes.

This is the horizon from which the creative mind frequently finds its way to the sublimation of poverty. 'Sublimation', we know, was Freud's term for the re-direction of repressed libidinal impulses. Base instinctual drives – toward practices like defecation, copulation, and murder (which, according to Freud, we all shamefully feel) – are reined in by the discipline of culture and with nowhere else to go, these energies are harnessed and turned towards more sublime goals – chief among them, art. In short, sublimation means the turning of the base, ugly, and distasteful into the sublime.

The current intellectual climate fosters the self-immolating gesture of taking one's brave stand against poverty in forms that enshrine it and even, in a sense, worship it. Official media and government strategists everywhere imply that the global periphery has ceased to matter to the economy's major players.[1] From this perspective, three quarters of the planet are not even worth exploiting any more and the real tragedy is that this fraction will be left to languish, irrelevant, while the rest of the world forges on in its quest for a transfigured, infinitely supple and de-centred laptop urbanism that has no need for national belonging or the rights and protections of citizenship. This way of thinking – which approximates the claims of neo-liberal globalisation – represents the current (updated and much-expanded) form of what used to be called multiculturalism. Earlier progressive moves to incorporate into the mainstream new subjectivities of race, place, and sexual preference have been transfigured into images of the largely non-white, culturally strange occupants of the peripheral countries of the world.

As a primarily U.S. export, globalisation rhetoric is an 'alpha' multiculturalism – in the sense of being virile, predatory, competitive and threatening – just the opposite, in fact, of that bid for increased tolerance and better access to employment and education that was first launched at the end of the nineteenth century in the revolutionary movements of Latin America. From those origins to now – via a u.s.-created dystopia of enforced immigration, enslavement and campaigns of extermination along the lines of skin colour, class, and exclusive faith – multiculturalism gradually took on the features of a boast.[2]

The term 'multiculturalism' is predicated on distinct national-cultural trajectories – a view lost on the celebrants of globalisation who say that nation-states are increasingly irrelevant relics in a world determined by transnational interests. Multiculturalism is politically ambiguous because, on the one hand, it has played the role of canon-buster and equaliser of opportunity and, on the other, it has allowed middle-class representatives of various ethnicities to flatter the self-portrait of America as a uniquely pluralist country. This flattery tends to lubricate the already well-oiled machine of globalisation discourse in which 'America' is cast as the mini-model of an inevitable world culture.

Another way this self-defeating aspect of imperial beneficence has expressed itself is in the form of a politico-exotic – a literary technique that extends an earlier erotic exoticism that was the preferred option in European travel narratives of the nineteenth century. This earlier rhetorical device has now lost its power to seduce contemporary audiences because its mechanisms of enchantment have been exposed and thoroughly criticized by two generations of postcolonial scholars. The politico-exotic, then, may be seen as an updating of imperial ideology, which is refreshed and replenished in the guise of a (rhetorical) "resistance" that is presented as having been enabled by the empire itself: as having been prompted by its exciting contradictions and limitless energies. Such an

approach functions more effectively as a defense of empire
since its credentials of resistance are 'obvious'.[3]

Caught in this morass of ideological contamination and
eager to pierce through to an ethical, human core, the artist is
drawn to racial otherness which has become, for complicated
historical reasons, ambiguous. The peripheral, the non-white
and the foreign can be beautiful and insurgent even while
being in harmony with imposing financial interests and
the most muscular of national governments. But, what are
the uses of an art that continues to derive its energies from
the image of third-world poverty as a way to inject new life
into a dying modernism? The third world – that diverse and
asymmetrical collection of underdeveloped countries whose
natural resources and labour are leached into the first world
– is also an *image* of poverty and, therefore, a valuable commodity. Although ethereal, its leverage (and profit potential)
is quite concrete.

Let us take a look at the image-function of the third world in more detail. *National Geographic* captured this perfectly in its special issue on Global Culture some years ago.

On the magazine's cover, an upper-class Indian mother, dressed in a sari, sits beside her Westernized daughter, dressed in shiny patent leather. There, crudely symbolised, sit two familiar oppositions: the traditional, expressed generationally as old age and therefore a sage and calm permanence associated with the culture of *place*, *versus* the modern, expressed as youth, globalisation, and the culture of *space*. The mother's benign maternal glance acts as a counterpoint to the daughter's steely, unsentimental and ambitious stare into the camera. As if parodying Gandhi's *swadeshi* movement against British imperialism (in which his countrymen were counselled to make homespun cloth as part of a boycott on British manufacture), the insouciant daughter has taken Indian production into her own hands, but in an MTV register. According to the photographic caption, the tight, black jumpsuit she wears is of 'her own design'. In place of the improvised resourcefulness of the proud colonial upstart, we are shown individualistic entrepreneurialism. Even as the mother projects a quiet professional dignity, the daughter intimates a subtle, and therefore acceptable, sexual availability through the tightness of her clothing and her slightly parted legs. Youth, sexuality and business-sense are here inextricable. In short, the photograph panders to a corporate ethos. Beneath the make-up and the created desire (which, depending on the viewer, might involve sex, fashion, or the exoticism of India, now whittled down to size), the multicultural shibboleths of globalisation – hybridity, opportunity, diversity, untrammeled contact, brave new creative forms, and technological wonders – are sold wholesale.

Within gallery culture and the world of the exhibition catalogue, I think it is fair to say that we have inherited the rarefied air of a political art whose best-known spokesperson in the post-ww ii era was probably Andy Warhol. For him, politics resided at the interface of public audience and marketing niche. Ironically acknowledging that all attempts to outmanoeuvre the logic of advertising were futile, he took refuge in stylish predictability, staying one step ahead of boredom by celebrating an ability to confess the impossibility of politics before being forced to do so by the police.

The legacy of Warhol has been altered without being fundamentally changed. Now, one moves deftly from gallery opening to loft party in the name of third world inclusiveness and expansiveness of artistic means – the default option of a political art figured as new. But, where is the art that captures the political actuality of the now? Where is that more brittle and less harmonious art capable of articulating at the level of value (and in the name of an appropriate concept of the beautiful), the inspirations, say, of the Hezbollah militant or the partisan of a Mexico City zocalo encampment protesting the recent fraudulent election that stole the presidency from Manuel Lopez Obrador? Where is the metropolitan art appropriate to the organisational bravery and contemporary (even futuristic) reminders of vibrant nations, regions, and cities evident in the civil wars that have erupted in Oaxaca, Caracas, Quito, Falluja, and Gaza?[4] Or is there, perhaps, no art worthy of capturing this reality? Is art itself powerless to reconcile such contradictions?

Of course, it is not the case that all artists are engulfed by a facile globo-speaking third-worldism, nor is it the case that portrayals of colonial themes or critiques of the West (and its images) are unthinkable today. The challenging work of contemporary artists like Monika Marklinger, Walid Raad, and Bill Wasik, for example, are impressive, intelligent, and politically adept.[5] Rather, my point is to underscore the uses of a philosophy of ambivalence that was linked to self-styled political art of the 1980's and, moreover, to see what connection that process has to the mixed blessing of today's multiculturalism.

Does the above image invite or resist criticism? It would be surprising if the latter because it is the work of the brilliant Brazilian photographer, Sebastiao Salgado whose career has been dedicated to exposing real-life, global inequality wrought by specific commercial and financial culprits. But this image's visual pun – its quotation of slender vertical form in dead tree and soon-to-be-dead boy – produces an odd sensation of disproportion between levity and horror. The ambiguity is arresting, especially as there can be no ambiguity of intention given Salgado's credentials. The problem, perhaps, rests with the demand to communicate to an audience indoctrinated by gallery culture and the seductive propaganda of globalisation.

This photograph by Salgado also works against itself, despite its formal balance and painful lyricism. The actual life of this woman may or may not be tragic – without a narrative caption, we cannot tell – but the disturbing aspect of the image is that it makes tragedy exquisite. We would not think of suspecting that the subject's posture and hand gestures were posed (that would be as manipulative and tasteless as the art of the mortician) but here art, as art, is incapable of escaping its negative function. To fulfil itself in arresting desire, this artwork is forced to contradict its intention of exposing an unpleasantness, the political solution for which can only exist in eradicating the conditions of the image itself. In this case, subtlety and form are an insult and being an artist implies collusion in delaying the eradication of such exquisite injustice. To be truly political means to refuse, at least temporarily, to be an artist.

By contrast, the poster for a recent film – *Workingman's Death* by Austrian filmmaker Michael Glawogger – portrays a multicultural panorama in five segments, on the experience of labourers in Russia, Indonesia, Haiti, Pakistan, and China. The accompanying advertising copy indicates its aesthetic placement:

[The director] shines his camera into five of the darkest, most grueling, environments of hard labor around the world in a deconstructive challenge to modern ideas of 'work'.

Without having to say so himself, Glawogger shows us in this brilliant day-in-the-life rendering that a great variety of lives have remained untouched by any sense of modern technological advancement and that worker's own understandings of their labors are deeply connected to notions of self, culture, and history. *Workingman's Death* has been widely acclaimed for its poetic cinematography and blatant capture of harsh realities.

By referring to the film's 'poetic cinematography' and 'deconstructive challenges', this passage seeks to distance the film from mere documentary. But this advertisement also bluntly clashes (in the most welcome fashion) with the cosmopolitan serenity of much of today's globo-theory, not only in denying that modern technologies are universally enjoyed, but also in moving the focus from being to doing. In place of the sensual surfaces of damaged bodies celebrated in philosophical registers, we are given the hidden and disparaged truth of the new global era: namely, the uses and abuses of labour.

What is more, in place of mute witness and enigmatic visuality, here the damaged lives of capitalism find their text. And this text – centred on the 'harsh realities' of work in the world's darkest places – reminds us of the limits of cosmopolitanism in both a colloquial sense and a more specialised one. In its everyday sense, cosmopolitanism means broad fellow-feeling, world travel, openness to cultural otherness and identification with peoples of different races, nations or cultures as equals. In this sense, cosmopolitanism stands as the opposite of nationalism, chauvinism or jingoism and so, to that degree, is an outlook most would endorse warmly. But the more appealing aspects of the term may also be cast in a more problematic light. In our new imperial era, cosmopolitanism suggests an ethos that is supposedly universally felt, without any limits placed on it by social status or location. In other words, the conditions of labour are not seen as barriers to recognition or understanding. The irresistibility of this new and broader claim for cosmopolitanism within the metropolitan countries has to do with its appearance of comporting (at the level of human value and ethics) with a demonstrable transformation in the material sphere, epochal changes in military, economic, and political arrangements, a new 'transnational moment'. But the problem with cosmopolitanism in this form is the mirage of the global in the local.

The silver lining in this cloud may be the fact that the myth of cosmopolitanism is, at last, wearing thin, and that the new universalism of rights and values it promised is finding its way to a limited realisation, against all info-age predictions, in those 'older' kinds of conflicts – mostly military, sometimes non-violent, but always disciplined and confrontational – occurring in the Middle East and Latin America. There has never before been a time when the emptiness of advertising, the structural inequality of free-market logic and the corruption of imperial power has been so obvious to so many. It is an age ripe for new *philosophes* to prepare the terrain in thought and artistic value for a radical reorganisation of society – a complete overturning – as opposed to the running-and-dodging operation of self-uncertainty that characterised the styles and moods of the 1980's and 1980's artworld. Art cannot make political change, but it can articulate a realm of value that nurtures, or draws positive attention to, that which can.

Meanwhile, in many parts of the still not fully colonised third world, cultural forms suggest the promise of a way of life that capitalism has not yet uprooted – the art of aimless conversation, the slowing of the pace of life, indifference to economic 'growth', hospitality, and the de-commercialisation of art (at least within limits). These are important psychological and emotional outlets for the negative energy overwhelming a metropolis characterised by the fear and restlessness of a productive system that would rather sublimate poverty than eradicate it.

Notes

1. This argument has been made by both enthusiasts and critics of globalisation. For the critical voices, see George Soros, *Open Society: Reforming Global Capitalism* (New York: Public Affairs, 2000); Joseph Stiglitz, *Globalization and its Discontents* (New York: W. W. Norton & Co., 2003); Jeremy Seabrook, *The No-Nonsense Guide to World Poverty* (London: Verso, 2004).

2. The classic statements of a much larger sentiment can be found in Domingo Faustino Sarmiento's *Facundo: Or, Civilization and Barbarism*, Mary Man, trans. (Harmondsworth, Middlesex: Penguin, 1998 [1868]), and in a more progressive, modern sense in José Martí's *Our America: Writings on Latin America and the Struggle for Cuban Independence,* Elinor Randall, Juan de Onís, and Roslyn Held Foner, trans. (New York: Monthly Review Press, 1977). Contrast these varied celebrations of the dignity and power of the mixed-race nation to the U.S. founding fathers. Discourse in the United States did not achieve these heights until the pragmatist philosophers adopted the new 'American' (of the Americas, that is) outlook to counter the eugenics movement at the turn of the century. For the latter story, see Richard Hofstadter, *Social Darwinism in American Thought* (New York: Braziller, 1955).

3. I examine the 'politico-exotic' in more detail in *At Home in the World: Cosmopolitanism Now* (Cambridge, MA: Harvard UP, 1997), 40–41, 180–199.

4. Thinking 'beyond the nation' is the call of much oppositional criticism in the art world at a time when the nation itself is frankly re-assertive. See, for example, the analysis of regime change in Venezuela, Bolivia, Argentina, and other countries in 'Amérique Latine rebelle', *Le Monde Diplomatique, Manière de Voir* 90 (December 2006–January 2007).

5. See *Beyond East and West: Seven Transnational Artists*, David O'Brien and David Prochaska, eds. Krannert Museum, University of Illinois-Champaign-Urbana (Urbana: University of Illinois, 2004) for the work of Raad. See also Bill Wasik, 'My Crowd', *Harpers* (March 2006) on Wasik's 'flash mob' art project.

INTERVIEW SERIES (2000)
VIDEOLOOP DVD, 6 MIN

Loulou Cherinet

During her studies at the University School of Fine Art & Design in Addis Abeba / Ethiopia Loulou Cherinet carried out a number of interview series. Together with a journalist friend she walked around her neighbourhood asking people the three questions we routinely ask most strangers: Where do you come from? How long have you been here? How do you like this place? The answers she receives shows variations of a theme, the emotions we attach to a nation, usually called nationalism or patriotism. Between the lines we can read a kind of monoculture where mobility is limited by social, economical and political realities.

#06
— How long have you
been here?
— I have never *been* to Ethiopia...
I grew up here in Ethiopia.
— Where do you come from?
— From my mother's stomach.
— How do you like it here?
— I was born here and now
I am here.

#21
— How long have you been here?
— A very long time... about
twenty-two years.
— Where do you come from?
— That's a very difficult question.
I cannot lie...
I have been here in Ethiopia all
this time...
— What do you think of Ethiopia?

— She's very good and thriving...
I love her.

#27
— How long have you been here?
— What do you mean?
I am not a stranger – you mean
since I was born?
I don't know... you are not sup-
posed to ask a woman her age...
I am very old.
— Where do you come from?
— I don't know. That question is
very difficult to answer... I guess
I slept in my mother's womb.
— What do you think of Ethiopia?
— She's so beautiful... such a
fertile country... but we also have
a little bit of poverty... she defi-
nitely makes us work hard.
I have nothing more to say.

— And where from?
— From here. I was born here,
over there, at Akaki hospital.
— What do you think of Ethiopia?
— I think she is wonderful.

#13
— How long have you been here?
— I am twenty-five years old.
That means I was born in Ethiopia
twenty-five years ago.
— Where do you come from?
— I was not born before I came
to Ethiopia. I was born… I mean
I spent nine months inside my
mother and then I came out.
Ever since then I have lived here.
— How do you like Ethiopia?
— I am very happy and proud to
be an Ethiopian. I love Ethiopia
very much… ok?

#17
— How long have you been in
Ethiopia?
— Twenty years.
— Where do you come from?
— From my mother.
— How do you like it here?
— How I like it here in Ethiopia?
I really like it… but I don't know.

#11
— How long have you been here?
— I was born in Ethiopia.
— Where do you come from?
— Here, I live here.

#23
— How long have you been in
Ethiopia?
— Fifteen years.
— Where do you come from?

— I came to Ethiopia… Well actually, before I knew that I was an Ethiopian I was just childish.
— What do you think of Ethiopia?
— I don't know. I don't think it's as good as people say. I mean… most things that people need to live well – we lack most of those things. That is not good. Thank you.

#25
— How long have you been here?
— In Ethiopia? Almost twenty-five years.
— Where do you come from?
— I am an Ethiopian citizen. I grew up here. I have never been abroad.
— What do you think of Ethiopia? How do you like it here?
— I see Ethiopia exactly as any other Ethiopian sees her. I mean, our love… The way we are born and raised together. Living together, that is the Ethiopian identity. We are unique. Wherever we live, wherever we go, we support each other. We respect our flag… These things make me happy – proud to be an Ethiopian. There are problems. One of our problems is that young people have no work. Except some of these difficulties… Solidarity… it is the solidarity that makes me happy to be an Ethiopian.

#8
— How long have you been in Ethiopia?
— I *am* in Ethiopia.
— Where do you come from?
— I used to stay with God.
— How do you like Ethiopia?
— Ethiopia is a very nice country.

#10

— How long have you been here?
— Thirty-one years.
— Where do you come from?
— From outside. Outside of Ethiopia. Not from this world. Maybe space…
— What do you think of Ethiopia?
— I don't *like* her. I try to under-stand her.

#35

— How long have you been here?
— I was born and grew up here. I went to school here. I'm not from anywhere.
— Where do you come from?
— From here, from Addis Ababa.
— What do you think of Ethiopia?
— You mean what I think of Ethiopia? Ethiopia… here in Ethiopia… No, I don't know. What was the question?
— Let me ask again, do you like Ethiopia?
— I have some good opinions about Ethiopia… regarding human rights and democracy…

#19

— How long have you been here in Ethiopia?
— Who, me? I was born here. I was born here and I grew up here.
— Where do you come from?
— I came out of my mother.
— What do you think of Ethiopia?
— Ethiopia is ok. It is a nice country. We have many different cultures, different people… I like that.

\#18

— How long have you been here in Ethiopia?

— I have been here almost twenty-five years.

— Where do you come from?

— My mother made me.

— How do you like it here?

— Ethiopia is our very, very unique and great motherland. You know, close to paradise… Anything else?

\#12

— How long have you been here?

— To begin with, I have never been out of Ethiopia so I can't say anything…

— Where do you come from?

— Well, that's the question… I mean, I have always been here, what kind of question is that?

— What do you think of Ethiopia?

— I have known her all my life. We have a strong culture that makes us proud. I love Ethiopia…

\#2

— How long have you been here?

— Seventy years.

— Where do you come from?

— I don't know. It is a mystery.

— What do you think of Ethiopia?

— I was born here. I grew up here. I have lived here…

\#15

— How long have you been here?

— Two years.

— Where do you come from?

— You can ask something else…

— Where do you come from?

— Your question is very difficult.

I don't have any answer…
— What do you think of Ethiopia?
— She is beautiful.

#22
— How long have you been here?
— Fifteen years.
— Where do you come from?
— One or two countries… Brazil,
I spent ten years there, then five
in Canada.
— How do you like Ethiopia?
— She is very beautiful… very.
Even before I left, Ethiopia has
always been great.

#26
— How long have you lived here?
— Twenty years.
— Where do you come from?
— America.

— And how do you like Ethiopia?
— She is beautiful, very beautiful.

#28
— When did you come to
Ethiopia?
— I was born here. I am an Ethio-
pian. Your question is strange…
— Where do you come from?
— Well, you have my first answer.
— What do you think of Ethiopia?
— Ethiopia is my mother, I know
her. I cannot discover her or have
opinions about her.

#30
— How long have you been here?
— I've been here from the
beginning.
— Where do you come from?
— I have been here all this time.

— How do you like Ethiopia?
— She's just fine. She's fine…

#33
— How long have you been here?
— I have been here all my life.
— Where do you come from?
— My mother gave birth to me.
Then I went to school. And finally
I got a job.
— What do you think of Ethiopia?
— I love Ethiopia very much.
I have lived in Ethiopia a long
time. She's rich; her nature is beau-
tiful, our people are working hard.
We have factories, and farmers…

#31
— How long have you been here?
— Me? I am an Ethiopian. I was
born and raised here. Some fifty
years ago…
— Where do you come from?
— I'm afraid I don't know
where… I was… maybe in heaven,
maybe being born…
— How do you like Ethiopia?
— My country is beautiful…
except our poverty and our own
laziness. I have been abroad so
I can compare. We have not fully
explored her. Still, we love her.

FROM ETHNICITY TO ETHICS

Hito Steyerl

During the end of 2005, the Bosnian city of Mostar became the second city in the world (After Hongkong) to have a Bruce Lee statue. It was unveiled in 2006 in the framework of a project called *De/construction of Monument* by the Sarajevo Center for Contemporary Art.

Bruce Lee statue in Mostar

Bosnia is not only vanguard in this regard, but also in regard to revealing the significance of European policies, among them the policy of multiculturalism; it is there that the internal contradictions and impossibilities of such policies are first revealed and yield irreconcilable dead ends. Far from presenting an image from an archaic past, the Balkan wars have actually proven to foreshadow a future in which culture, rather than politics, is regarded as a sufficient reason to trigger massive conflict.

The Bruce Lee project in Mostar was, at least to my interpretation, not a cultural project; rather, it was an exercise in getting rid of culture in order, finally, to be able to breathe again. The monument was not built in reverence either to Lee's cultural affiliation or to Martial arts (whatever culture that might represent), but because Lee is a person who appeals to members of all the so-called ethnicities in Bosnia – that is to say Croats, Serbs, Muslims, Gypsies, Jews and so on. The breadth of his appeal arises not because he incorporates any specific culture, but because he embodies values like honesty, hatred of corruption, loyalty, friendship and a sense of justice which, according to the producers of the statue, are severely lacking in Bosnia and beyond. Thus, this statue symbolises a significant step away from the rhetorics of recognition of difference in Bosnia, where existing segregation is enforced and upheld. This public artwork transcends ethnicity in the quest for a new ethics, demonstrating that Bosnia is not only avant-garde in relation to the dystopia of a deeply segregated country which it represents, but also in regard to the search for ways to overcome the rhetorics of discrimination and segregation.

Bosnia is also at the forefront of 'ethnic marketing', which is perhaps to be expected in a place where one and the same language is marketed as three different languages which, in turn, support three different educational systems, two and a half administrations, fourteen regional parliaments and 400 ministers. Thus, inventing different cultures is not only a matter for the imagination, but also a factor of economics, at least for the respective elites of those cultures. If the same principle were applied to a hotel room, four different prices would need to be charged for the same thing. Perhaps – from a materialist perspective – this is the principle of multiculturalism: to market the same under different brand names and charge different prices.

Advertisement in Sarajevo

Because multiculturalism is so firmly entrenched in the organisation of the state and administration, I believe that there is hardly a better place from which to gain insight into the phenomenon of multiculturalism than contemporary Bosnia. Maybe this is also the best place to look for ways to overcome the consequences of segregationist multiculturalism. Let me try to describe what I mean by using the example of a project I am currently working on which has the working title 'Archive of Lost Objects' – dealing as it does with the reconstruction of those lost objects – and is an investigation into the paradoxes of documentary forms intended as an example of how culture annihilates art.

While working on this project, Boris Buden and I have repeatedly encountered the disappearance of modernist, trans-ethnic, secular cultural institutions of the 1980's, most radically during the war in the 1990's which took place throughout former Yugoslavia. One of those institutions is the Film Museum in Sarajevo; it is a classic ex-socialist municipal institution, set up to preserve all film productions made in Bosnia and Herzegovina and to promote artists' films. Operating under severe financial constraints, it is run down but still functioning. During the war, it was hit twice by grenades and a large part of the film stock was either lost during those attacks or used for heating during the war, as the film burns well. As a result of heroic efforts from the staff and great support from the Yugoslav Film Museum in Belgrade, almost all the prints have been retrieved since the war and, with the collection restored, the museum still screens films (albeit sometimes under quite unusual conditions). When Boris Buden and I arrived there in the middle of the day, a famous partisan film called the *Battle of the Neretva* was screening in a completely empty cinema. In this film, Tito is played by Richard Burton and the main fascist and tchetnik arch-villains are played by Yul Brynner and Orson Welles. The projectionist had vowed that he would screen each film once a year, even if there was no audience, in order to ventilate them and prevent further decay.

To return to the missing object in question: despite all efforts at conservation without any real means, a few films from the collection remain missing, having been irretrievably lost during the war. Of the early monthly film journals made in Bosnia and Herzegovina after WWII – usually screened before the main feature to provide selected news about the socialist production efforts, the construction of tractors, the inauguration of new factories and so on – the first, second and twentieth journal are missing.

These journals were filmed on Nitro stock, which burns very easily and, for this reason, they had to be stored in a bunker located in a film studio on the edge of town. During the first phase of the siege of Sarajevo in 1992, this studio found itself in a no-mans-land between two frontlines. As the studio has two entrances, it could be accessed from both the Serbian and Bosnian sides. People from the Serbian side were informed about the prints and evacuated them to a nearby house on the Serbian side owned by a man called Džoki ; but, this act of retrieval had been witnessed by someone on the Bosnian frontline, the house of Džoki was hit by a grenade and went up in flames.

When we asked the director of the archive, Devleta Filipovic from the Film Museum, which scene from this lost film (Journal NO. 1) she would like to reconstruct in the framework of our project, her answer was absolutely clear: she chose a scene, filmed shortly after WW11, which shows illiterate women learning their alphabet. This scene shows how literacy classes were organised for elderly rural people, particularly Muslim women. The teacher, who was usually very young, stood in front of a blackboard and taught the veiled women how to read and write; this was the scene she and her colleague Halid Bunic wanted to reconstruct for the project.

This brief scene shows a cultural institution, strongly imbued with modernist and democratic values, an institution which educates and empowers women, which is deeply secular and, at least theoretically, culturally blind. Of course, not only this film has disappeared, but also many of the political values which went along with it. The grenade which destroyed this film also symbolically destroyed the socialist-modernist ideal of education and empowerment of women in secular institutions, as imperfect as they may have been. It marked the beginning of cultural institutions being segregated along religious and ethnic lines, which also concerns the institution of the Film Museum itself.

To confirm the story of the disappearance of the film, we went to Pale, one of the administrative seats of Bosnian Serbs, who, in the meantime, have established their own Film Museum. Both museums – the one from Sarajevo and the one from Pale, which are located about 20 km apart – were in contact for the very first time through this project. Not only are these film museums segregated, but this segregation also produces very unusual institutions, like the Film Museum in Pale, which has neither a screening facility nor any films on stock. This is a cultural institution in the most radical form, as it produces its own ethnicity and, instead of actual films – which have been destroyed or were never produced in the first place – we have the separatist institution of national cinematographies. And, in the place of the old ideals of empowering women, there is an increased domestication of women, either by religious, cultural or capitalist means, the latter by virtue of Bosnia becoming one of the pivotal points for trafficking women.

Of course this destruction of a publicly-funded cultural sphere – which, at least in theory, adhered to modernist or, more broadly, Enlightenment values like education, equality and empowerment – mirrors a trend seen everywhere. In Bosnia, the welfare state has been under attack not only from market-driven neo-liberalism but also from nationalist indigenisms which aimed at restricting artistic freedom in the process of implementing religious values and constructing new national cultures.

Let me give you another example of the dissolution of a multiethnic public sphere, which took place at a very charismatic location in Sarajevo: a memorial park in a part of town called Vraca. The park contains a small fortress from the Ottoman period, which was also in use during Austro-Hungarian rule. After WWII, this fortress was transformed into a museum for the liberation fighters – that is, for the antifascists who had been killed during the war – and the names of more than 10.000 people were written in plaster letters on the walls of two courtyards. This monument, located precisely on the border between the Bosnian-Croatian Federation and the Serbian Republic, was completely devastated during the war. In fact, it was the first location from which an attack on Sarajevo was launched as it is situated on a hill overlooking the city. During the war, the soldiers stationed there erased the partisan names on the walls by shooting at them with machine guns; most of the letters fell to the ground to shatter irreparably. The few remaining form a strange, illegible text, a hieroglyph for a liberation from fascism which has literally lost its meaning.

View of the memorial park in Vraca

I picked up some of these shattered letters and asked myself what sort of story is behind each of them. At the same time, I try to resist the temptation to reconstruct their original meaning. This is not about the restoration of some sort of original text, or the mourning of its disappearance or about nostalgia for a lost story compared to the coherence of modernism. In my opinion, these letters mean something completely different.

To come back to Vraca; the main value under attack here is the antifascist consensus which was achieved, at least on the surface, throughout Europe after WWII. With the coming to power of right wing populist parties in Austria and Denmark, with the rise of neo-fascist and separatist organisations and with the rise of new paradigms of totalitarianism – particularly in the new Europe, which claim that Stalinism and Fascism are basically the same – this consensus has been shattered. The destruction of Vraca, and the 10.000 names which were written on the walls there, is a symbol of this breakdown. However, despite a desperate lack of funds in Bosnia, this institution is going to be reconstructed next year, a process which poses another problem to which I will return.

What would be the solution to the problem of an excess of culture and segregation? How should we conceptualise the production of new public spheres and of a commonality? Here, several problems arise. The first fact is that it is no longer possible to go back to the old form of modernist cultural institution; we can neither reconstruct the literacy classes nor even, I would argue, the memorial park of Vraca. Of course, it is physically possible to reconstruct it – Vraca can be re-built. But, in a political context in which most of the values for which those partisans fought – as part of a multiethnic, secular, socialist society – are increasingly irrelevant, perhaps even considered crazy and dangerous, and the people who believe in them are marginalised as freaks, a reconstructed Vraca will be a shell without content. In a society in which most cultural institutions, including schools, are segregated along ethnic and religious lines, Vraca has lost its meaning. It is also especially absurd in a context in which three different textbooks are issued to teach the same language and this procedure, along with the segregation of schools, is backed by the minority rights regulations of the European Union.

A similar problem arises with the reconstruction of the literacy classes. In a context in which women can largely read and write, but are being commodified by traffickers, literacy classes miss the point. Of course, they can still exist, but, if women are using their literacy skills to sign contracts which force them into debt bondage, the emancipation which literacy promised remains remote.

The problem that we cannot reconstruct – the lost sense of common purpose, which it is impossible to excavate or retrieve – is the problem we are dealing with in our project. It is impossible to recreate this institution, but this impossibility does not have to lead to mourning or melancholy or nostalgia. In our project, we are trying to recreate very accurate documents about these lost institutions from the memories of two witnesses. In the case of the lost film from Sarajevo Film Museum, the director of the museum and the projectionist were asked to contribute to the documentary reconstruction of the scene of the literacy classes for women. How did each person reconstruct this scene? How did a police draftsman depict the reconstruction of the scene they had described from their memories? This is the account given by one witness:

First version of literacy class

According to the laws of producing documentary evidence, it had to be two witnesses, because one witness is no witness as they say. You need two witnesses in order to produce evidence; everything else is hearsay. This was also the method used by the Bosnian authorities to restore documents to people who lost them during the war. They needed two witnesses to prove their identity. But – and this is the paradox – if you have two witnesses, you also have two quite different memories.

Second version of literacy class

You see that both witnesses remember different things and, at the moment at which the document becomes 'objective' – because it is confirmed by two witnesses – it also becomes contradictory. This becomes apparent in the video we made from the process of drawing from memory, which simply documents creative confabulation. In short: at the same moment a document becomes a document it also becomes a fiction and the lost objects we are reconstructing are both objective and fictitious, both true and confabulated. They become themselves only through this constitutive difference.

Now the reconstruction process becomes interesting because it is no longer about uncovering a lost truth from the past, but about inventing a new truth which comes from the future. We realised that these memories were only partly based on the lost film – in fact, the projectionist flatly stated that he never saw the film – and partly pieced together from personal memory and feature films; generally speaking, they were less about what the scene was really like and more about *how the scene should have been.*

In fact, the witnesses had not invented the literacy class they had seen in the past, but the literacy class they wanted to have in the future, which would be opposed to the reactionary processes of indigenisation of the present. Using all the standard 'truth procedures' for the construction of a documentary and forensic means of reconstruction, something interesting had happened: a sort of creative fictionalisation was produced.

What does all of this now mean for the future of the institution? As I said before, it does not make sense to reconstruct the literacy class from the film journal in its original form because its social context has been lost, as has the one in Vraca. But what about inventing a new literacy class, which would no longer try to restore the original meaning of those broken letters from Vraca, to reconstruct the names and stories which were originally represented by those letters? This literacy class would encourage its pupils to read the text in its fragmented and shattered form; it would have to invent a language which makes sense of this new form of writing. There is no lost meaning to reconstruct in those letters because the meaning is already manifested in the fact of their fragmentation. In our new literacy class, we cannot identify with the teacher anymore, we must identify with the students in their task of inventing a new language. Those broken letters from Vraca represent the total fragmentation of all spheres of life in late capitalism, a fragmentation which is often equivalent to destruction and also very often expressed in the form of culture. This fragmentation must be acknowledged at once because there is no way back to the original unity. At the same time, it must be opposed because we can only decipher it in a new common language.

We have to learn to write those letters, not by restoring their original meaning but by inventing a new one and, with it, a new language of emancipation. And, if there is an emancipatory role for a cultural – let alone a multicultural – imagination, then it is to participate in inventing this new form of literacy.

BIOSWOP.NET

Natascha Sadr Haghighian

bioswop.net is an internet platform for CV-exchanges where artists and other cultural practitioners can borrow and lend CV's for various purposes. *bioswop.net* went online in October 2004 and is a work in process. The aim is to have more and more people exchange their cv's for representational purposes such as catalogues, etc. The project aims for even more redundancy regarding this aspect of artistic production, in order to finally undermine the purpose of the cv, and also for the sake of better entertainment.

www.bioswop.net

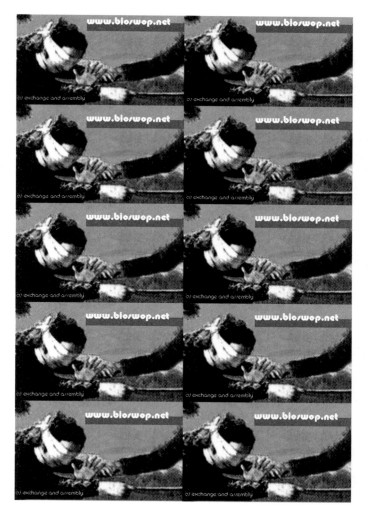

AN 'AESTHETICISATION OF POLITICS'?
ASSESSING PERSPECTIVES ON
EUROPEAN CONTEMPORARY ARTS FUNDING,
STATE-CORPORATISM,
AND LATE CAPITALIST CULTURE
IN A NEW AGE OF EMPIRE

Jonathan Harris

Passaic centre loomed like a dull adjective. Each 'store' in it was an adjective unto the next, a chain of adjectives disguised as stores... Actually, Passaic had no centre – instead it was a typical abyss or an ordinary void. What a great place for a gallery! Or maybe an 'outdoor sculpture show' would pep that place up!

Robert Smithson,
'A tour of the monuments of Passaic,
New Jersey' (1967)[1]

The symposium *A Fiesta of Tough Choices* held in Stockholm in March 2006, along with other recent international conferences, addressed the situation that the visual arts have got themselves into since the rise of 'cultural policy as social policy' in the western nation-states. Fiesta, or 'festivalisation' – an ambiguous name for something which is good *and* bad evoking, on the one hand, images of 'pepped-up' pleasures, even abandon, and, on the other, implying a kind of ('arms length') manipulation, or puppetry, controlled by actors known and unknown – might be thought of as a refraction of multiculturalism: a concept, ideology, and state policy now requiring urgent reconsideration.

Although the origins and development of cultural policy as social policy, in different countries in western Europe, correspond to specific features within those societies, it is possible to identify the same basic story: the adoption by national and local governments of the conviction that some things called 'culture' and 'the arts' may act as effective vehicles, or levers, for desired social change. In every western European country, there are now many organisations, at different levels in both state and private sectors, which have an interest in public art and in the claims being made for it by government officials and politicians as an instrument in determining social policy. In England, for instance, a lot has been heard recently on the role of culture and the arts in 'promoting citizenship' and achieving things called 'social cohesion' and 'social inclusion'. In Liverpool at the moment – with 2008 'Capital of Culture' status saturating public policy and rhetoric in the city – the overarching call to arms – with nothing 'arms length' about it – is Regeneration.

This is a term that has also dominated the language of governments across Europe, and far beyond, since at least the 1960's. It has a range of meanings – some literal and some metaphorical – and some senses, indeed, that escape the intentions of the technocrats, politicians, and armies of advisers in public institutions who rely on it. Regeneration actually implies a continuous *cycle* of fortunes – with an inevitable phase of death and infertility. For instance, in biology, generation and regeneration is an *autochthonous* process

– that is, it has its own systemic, self-regulating order; it is nature. To apply the term to social policy is to appropriate a labile, slippery metaphoric field of references whose meanings and implications might invade, or corrupt, the new territory in dangerous and unpredictable ways. Interestingly, regeneration – like terms such as 'resurgence' and 'renaissance' – has a particular history of use within fascist discourses of the early-twentieth century. Regeneration then resurfaced in the period after WWII, with governments since 1945 couching their neo-corporatist populism in 'liberal-democratic' rather than fascistic terms. And, instead of ideological interpellation organised around notions of national or ethnic identity – as in Germany and Italy under the Nazis and the Fascisti – modern European states have relied upon notions of citizenship, social solidarity and, more recently, multiculturalism.

Rhetorics of 'urban regeneration' – often brought about through economic investment by combined state and capitalist agencies – and of 'social regeneration' through the arts (the two usually bound up together in practice) create a powerful, though unstable, set of assumptions. This high-sounding meshing of values and beliefs is nonetheless rather fragile because those individuals, groups, and organisations constituting the art world frankly don't all pull in the same direction. Multiculturalism is a significant conceptual node in this network of assumptions, values, and beliefs – related in important ways to theories and practices of regeneration – and is now also caught up in the global politics of what might be called 'fundamentalist threat' and 'fundamentalist counter-threat'. By dint of this situation – which has been enhanced dramatically since 9/11 and the 'War on Terror' declared by U.S. President George Bush and UK Prime Minister Tony Blair – the art world finds itself in the most politicised of wider worlds. Not since the Cold War of the 1950's and 1960's and, before that, the time of the Popular Front against fascism in the 1930's have artists and their varied intermediaries and interlocutors had to face (or try to avoid) the difficult questions of how artistic work, aspirations, and interests might be, or should be, ideologically exploited.

Of course, those questions are also begged (and yet often evaded) by the terms and ideology of multiculturalism. This shibboleth of western liberal social-democratic politics and policy has existed for so long now that only fractions on the extreme right and left have, until very recently, ever made any attempt to question it. While their contributions were ruled out of 'reasonable' debate, they were, in a way, simultaneously integral to defining it: if only the rump of neo-fascists and a handful of anarchists opposed the ideas of state-enforced tolerance, racial harmony and pluralistic democracy, this was held as conclusive evidence that a broad centrist consensus must rightfully occupy the philosophical and moral high ground.

A reconceptualisation of the constituencies making up the art world now needs to be attempted in order to reconsider the nature of this contemporary *juste milieu*. The globalised, corporatised art world is made up of specialists, networkers, agents and experts, labouring in many areas, across a wide range of institutions, and responsible for a vast range of products and services. Artists, on the whole, still make the artworks, but agency administrators in both state and private sectors increasingly draw-up funding, sponsorship, and commissioning initiatives. These agencies might be local, national or transnational – as there is now a stratum of artists, administrators, and freelance curators moving around the world permanently (electronically or in aeroplanes), determining biennial themes and commissioning projects, advising local staff and delivering papers on the purposes and values of their particular art world product.

All these phenomena are part of the new institutions defining the political economy of contemporary art, but not all (or even most) of these elements are novel. Arguably a new arrangement, or *configuration*, of these elements, along with an enormous expansion in their scale, has emerged since the early 1990's. In addition, this art world is now itself a structural component of, or node within, the globalised capitalist economy. Globalisation, too, has a much longer history, though the term became orthodox – supplanting others such as 'world system', 'imperialism', 'colonialism' and even 'postmodernity' – only about fifteen years ago.

Events and new organisational rules and regularities in this contemporary art world have radically outstripped the preconceptions of the groups of specialists – the art critics and art historians – hitherto responsible for making sense of contemporary art and artistic production. Unlike what might be called the new administration class in the globalised art world – with their interests tied ideologically and materially to such state doctrines as multiculturalism and regeneration as well as to capitalist 'added value' thinking – critics and art historians have traditionally maintained (or been allotted) a relative autonomy in terms of their professional identities and activities. Those critics and art historians working in the universities continue to enjoy a degree of autonomy, in terms of what may be said, that far exceeds that of most other art world professionals; yet it might reasonably be concluded that, as a group, they have a corresponding powerlessness to bring about change or influence events in the art world. Often called 'commentators', this term implies a position *outside* of the system, although, increasingly during the twentieth century, some kinds of art historians became *integrated* into the complex and often obscure dynamics of the art market. Their connoisseurship, paid for by the dealers, and their publishing activities affected the economic and aesthetic value attributed to artists and artworks.

But *most* art historians and critics concerned with twentieth century and contemporary art maintain a vocabulary and a set of aptitudes drawn from the discourses of modernism and what Peter Bürger, amongst others, called the Theory of the Avant-Garde.[2] That is, they still operate with a notion of art, of artistic production and ontologies of value in art drawn from the paradigm of early-twentieth century artistic movements. Their concerns are with individual artists, with meaning understood as a function of authorial intent and critical deliberation, over the highly-wrought, complex, multivalent surfaces and substances of artworks and their fields of inter-reference with other works. (Incidentally, on the whole, this applies as much to postmodernist art, in all its hybridities, as it does to standard modernist paintings and sculptures.)

So, the two broad groups of intellectuals that comprise the professional class of the art world – let us call them the 'agency administrators' and the 'commentators' – are both, in different ways, excluded (and self-excluded) from critical analysis of the now-dominant system of support for art as a vehicle of cultural policy. The agency administrators have some *practical* concepts, for example 'patronage', 'creativity' and 'public'. Of course these agency administrators have working notions of these, and others. Their definitions are limited to how they fit into the commissioning briefs. These concepts are necessary to operate within this system, but the agency administrators have not – and arguably *cannot* because of their material interests – convert them into *theoretical*, and hence critical, concepts. There is, then, no existing, powerful critical discourse (in the Foucauldian sense of ideas, texts, institutions, practices, rules and regulations) that can make adequate sense of this new situation.

Critical insight *is* sometimes possible and capable of being provided by some people within the professional art world class. The Stockholm conference offered the possibility for some of the functionaries, players, and commentators to think aloud about the system and its opportunities and pitfalls.

There is another subgroup within the art world system: the artists themselves. Where do artists stand in relation to critical insight, and in relation to both the work of agency administrators and commentators? Obviously, they too have a lot of interest in a system which already does, or may in the future, provide them with a livelihood and some economic security. Artists are, of course, ideologically pivotal to the declared purposes of the system. Shop-worn and yellowed at the edges as these myths might be, artists can still represent potent fantasies of freedom, creativity, agency, cultivation (and even sometimes critical insight itself). Drawn from modernist discourse and earlier, artists adhere to still-influential paradigms of value and meaning in human production. Within both state and private sector investment strategies, their artworks are made to stand for added value of various kinds – social and cultural interventions into what are called 'communities' and 'markets', for which, in the main, read: 'business communities' and 'communities of consumers'. In Britain combined public/private funding packages is now the norm for major capital projects such as hospitals and schools. For attracting new industry and businesses to its regions (such as the new retail quarter being built in Liverpool for 2008, apparently the biggest building site development in Europe) – regeneration partly means a re-packaging and re-branding of artists and their artworks.

What, finally, of multiculturalism? Where do this term, ideology and set of practices fit into the art world system? Well, it obviously motivates and underpins notions of *who* might make, and benefit from, artworks. Multiculturalism is inseparable from what might be called 'community-ism' – another key term within the standard rhetoric of politicians and administrators who wish to invoke, suggest or designate tangible senses of integrated society and organic 'social relationships'. Community always *sounds* like a real place, or a shared sense of belonging or meaning. It also implies interests-in-common and bonds based on family, religion or cultural background. The nineteenth century German sociologist, Ferdinand Tönnies, made an important distinction between community, in this strong sense *(gemeinschaft)*, and mere, mechanical 'association' or 'society' for private interest or advantage *(gesellschaft)*. He was drawing a contrast between two kinds, or ideas, of social order – the former small-scale, perhaps rural, and the latter city-based and clearly commercial/capitalist. *Gesellschaft* could, and would if allowed to dominate, destroy the bonds and meanings of *gemeinschaft*.

Contemporary state-ideological use of community-ism and multiculturalism attempts to fight against the irresistible logic of Tönnies's argument and against the history of capitalism itself. Given that we in Europe live in state-capitalist societies – in which the state exists quixotically in order both to guarantee and, at the same time, ameliorate the social effects of advanced global monopoly capitalism – it is of no surprise that an ideal of community remains a significant hope and wager, designed to try to create the thing it claims already exists. Cultural policy as social policy – festivalisation – is one tactic in this wager. Yet, in this war of ideological forms of proposed social belonging, *actual* community is under strong, perhaps even destructive, pressure from *abstracted* national and now international senses of order and action. In Britain, the U.S. and elsewhere, national or federal laws designed to 'prevent terror', curtailing freedoms of speech and assembly, have interrupted community (already a very fragile, endlessly-decomposing and recomposing ideological-experiential entity) by imposing upon it the necessarily abstract force of what is called 'national emergency'.

Multiculturalism and public arts funding are *reconfigured* within this world at local, national, and international levels – in terms of both policy practices and ideological articulation. Artists employed, and artworks produced, under the banner of 'multiculturalism' under the conditions of 'national emergency' *will* bear the imprint of this situation, though it will

not really or usually be saliently expressed visually or themati-
cally. This is why most art critics and historians will be of little
use in developing the analysis needed to make sense of art in
this new age of Empire. It will, paradoxically, produce both
what Walter Benjamin called an 'aestheticisation of politics'
– a massaging or sublimation of the contradictions and struggles within the social polity – and its opposite, what he called
(dreaming of socialism, remember) 'the politicisation of aesthetics'– a de-sublimation and manifestation of contradiction
and struggle.[3] But, under the present conditions, this will not
be a political visualisation of a critique of capitalism and fascism, or a political visualisation or thematisation exploring a
future radically-changed society. It will, unfortunately, much
more likely be an extension of what has already happened: the
'policy-fication' of art as a tool of social manipulation and the
increasing integration of art world professionals into a global
neo-liberal political and state-capitalist bureaucracy.

Notes

1. Jack D. Flem (ed.) *Robert Smithson: The Collected Writings*/Berkeley:
University of California Press, 1996, 68–74.

2. Peter Bürger, *Theorie der Avantgarde*, (Frankfurt: Suhrkamp, 1974);
later published as Bürger, Peter. *The Theory of the Avant-Garde*, transl.
Michael Shaw (Minneapolis: University of Minnesota Press, 1984).

3. Walter Benjamin, 'The Work of Art in the Age of Mechanical
Reproduction', in H. Arendt (ed.) *Illuminations* (London: J. Cape, 1970),
219–2264; reprinted in F. Frascina and C. Harrison (eds.) *Modern Art and
Modernism: A Critical Anthology* (London: Harper and Row/The Open
University, 1986), 217–220.

NEW WORD ORDER
ON THE SUBLIMINAL POWER OF WORDS

Måns Wrange

"My job is to look for the words that trigger the emotion. Words alone can be found in a dictionary or a telephone book, but words with emotion can change destiny, can change life as we know it. We know it has changed history; we know it has changed behavior; we know that it can start a war or stop it. We know that words and emotion together are the most powerful force known to mankind."

Frank Luntz,
political consultant and pollster

The Foucauldian notion of language as power is by now well known, but single words can equally have considerable impact. Words can launch new phenomena and pinpoint neglected identities, and many of the words we use on a daily basis did not appear spontaneously, but are increasingly the result of effective lobbying campaigns.

The U.S. Republican Party, for example, has been particularly successful in using specific words and phrases in order to trigger specific responses. The master of such spin doctoring is the pollster Frank Luntz, and one noted outcome of his strategy is the Bush administration's use of the neutral sounding term 'climate change' instead of 'global warming'.

Sweden equally has a long tradition of inventing new words for political reasons. A current example is 'lifepuzzle' (livspusslet), used to designate the difficulties of combining a career with a satisfactory personal life. The word, also used in the media during election campaigns, was created by the Swedish special interest group TCO (The Swedish Confederation of Employees), who have registered it as a trademark.

Not seldomly, euphemisms are introduced in Swedish to eradicate unwanted associations of class, gender or ethnicity. For the last ten years, the center and right wing parties have, for example, promoted tax relief for 'close household services' (hushållsnära tjänster) – a less loaded term than 'maid' or 'cleaner'.

It is especially when it comes to labeling identity that words can have great political impact. For the last decade, Sweden has been engaged in a discussion on how to refer to immigrants. Terms like 'second-' or 'third generation immigrants' are frequently used even for people who have lived their whole lives in Sweden. Recent studies show that the term 'immigrant' is mostly used in relation to problems in society such as drugs, criminality and social exclusion, and in an attempt to avoid these social stigmas, the authorities have introduced a whole range of alternatives. Such as 'new Swedes' (nya svenskar), 'foreign-born persons' (utlandsfödda personer) and 'persons with a foreign background' (personer med utländsk bakgrund). However, none of these labels have been successful, neither as everyday terms, nor as efforts to alter the negative connotations. The Swedish authorities have yet to hire spin doctors like Karl Luntz.

The Revolutionary Word Experiment is a project which has enlisted the help of pollsters and experts in rhetoric, copywriting, literature and media theory, in the process of which a new word is constructed. By combining product placement, word-of-mouth marketing, branding and political spin doctoring, the invented word is disseminated within the population to make its way into the Swedish language.

PROJECT DESCRIPTION OF THE REVOLUTIONARY WORD EXPERIMENT (2007)

Måns Wrange

The Revolutionary **WORD**® Experiment

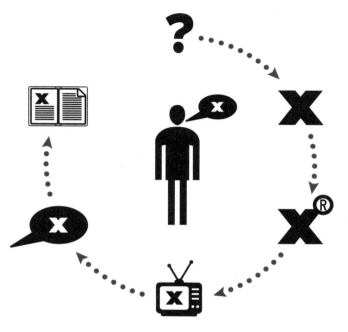

Focus groups are conducted to determine the need for a new word.

The word is constructed in collaboration with experts from the disciplines of rhetoric, copywriting and literature.

The word is trademarked to prevent it from being commercially exploited.

The word is disseminated with the cooperation of influential media personalities, who use the word in public contexts.

The word enters the common vocabulary after people begin using it in everyday conversation.

The word is listed in dictionaries. As a result, the trademark protection disappears and the word enters the public domain.

Måns Wrange/Ombud
www.ombud.org

MULTICULTURALISM IS BETTER THAN MONOCULTURALISM; POSTCOLONIALISM IS BETTER THAN COLONIALISM. REJOICING IN A FIESTA OF TOUGH CHOICES

Tirdad Zolghadr

A friend of mine, who lives and works in Basle, was walking home from the supermarket one day when she encountered a striking neighbourhood scene. An old Swiss couple was standing on their first floor balcony, showering a Tamil girl in racist insults. The six-year-old was standing by a flowerbed, from which she had stolen an impressive white rose. My friend intervened. 'Come on folks, don't get worked up,' she calmly told the old-age pensioners. 'You'll die off anyway – won't be long now.'

I think there are three very positive things to say about this gesture. First of all, the strategic benefit – the shock-and-awe efficiency with which peace and quiet was achieved. Secondly, the choice of confrontation over mediation or dialogue – liberal or otherwise – is something which takes more political courage than I can usually muster. Thirdly, the gesture touches on an ageist prejudice we all tacitly share: the subconscious hope of gradually slouching toward something better, more enlightened, through the generations. At the risk of generalisation, I think we all realise, to varying degrees, that this is not actually happening. On the contrary, generation after generation of voters are showing substantial moves toward nationalism. Orientalist paradigms are getting bigger and better by the day, with Hollywood movies, news reports and military incursions demonstrating softer, and thus more resilient, forms of racialised packaging than before. And new models of multiculturalism – from Fortress Europe to the open-door policies found elsewhere – are seldom encouraging and lead to rather ferocious forms of exploitation and cultural nostalgia.

To make things yet more trying, with the United States unduly influencing the perception of multicultural models worldwide, many shun the term multiculturalism because of its imperialist subtext. Mentioning multiculturalism often has the same effect as saying 'George W. Bush' or 'Santiago Sierra', prompting everyone in the room to roll their eyes at the ceiling, then scramble to congratulate each other on their shrewd sense of political finesse. By and large, people across the political spectrum agree that it is this perception of multiculturalism that needs to fall out of favour in order for 'tolerance', or perhaps something better, to emerge and develop.

Özan Sinan, founder of LabOne Urban & Ethnic Marketing Agency in Berlin, once quipped that 'as long as a society claims it's multicultural, it simply is not.'[1] One cannot help but wonder whether this maxim also implies its opposite, that societies which are more discreetly multicultural – like the understated pluralistic society found in Tehran – are actually more genuinely diverse. More importantly, this phrase suggests that multiculturalism inherently signifies a lack, or crisis, real or imagined – rather than a truly existent or inexistent state of affairs – an ideal, the conceptual purity of which is confined to the decision-makers. One can extrapolate from this, as Slavoj Zizek has repeatedly done, to argue that the most rabid forms of racism known to modernity are a consequence of the inherently disingenuous, essentialist terminology of multiculturalism itself. This posits ethnic violence as a direct consequence of modernism, with its nationalistic modes of belonging, rather than a resurgence of anything primitive.

Not just confined to a societal model, multiculturalism may also be considered as a discursive apparatus, precisely by virtue of the irreconcilable incongruities it brings to the fore. If its use is brutally capricious, this need not mean that it is irrelevant. Postcolonial writing, for instance, offers a dual characterisation of the term 'culture', as either a trap of exotic outsiderhood, or as a politicised contention that reason cannot be monopolised. This becomes rather poignant in the context of the *2006: Year of Cultural Diversity* in Sweden and similar initiatives. How can one possibly prompt any culturalised contentions from above? The Social Democratic idea, according to former Minister of Culture and Education, Leif Pagrotsky, was to '(...)motivate people who seldom visit state financed cultural institutions [to] visit, get involved and relate to the activity.' Surely, for a non-nativist contention to emerge, one would need to re-examine the imperatives of 'motivation', 'involvement' and 'activities'? Project Co-ordinator, Yvonne Rock, added 'Knowledge is power. Culture is power as well. But the power of expression is not given to all of us. Nor is the power to feel connected through culture. We must strive towards a cultural life where both social and cultural equality prevails.' She argued for as many individuals as possible to be '(...)heard, seen and present in culture and society.'[2]

Rather than bemoan yet another mistake by the Left, I would prefer to underline that such top-down initiatives by the Swedish Executive have less in common with postcolonial ambitions than with brash, free-market meritocracy. Compare this with the 'Mighty-is-the-Mongrel' approach of U.S. economist Richard Florida, who argues that multiculturalism is, quite simply, good for your city, your neighbourhood, and your institution, as an asset in the global marketplace for locations, localities and local flavours. Florida's seminal publication, *The Rise of the Creative Class,* offers statistical proof of metropolises with a higher degree of ethnic diversity being more successful in attracting business because, he argues, the ambiance they foster is attractive to creative types who, in turn, are essential to productivity and innovation. Interestingly, Florida also demonstrates that cities with 'high creative density' have the highest number of stress disorders and the largest inequalities of income since creative labour is heavily dependent on poorly-paid service work; cultural diversity thus becomes a meritocratic way of dividing labour.[3]

Unlikely as it seems, Richard Florida openly suggests that class is the most pernicious blind spot in multicultural debate. The widespread denial of the very existence of class, at a time of unprecedented economic disparities, is striking but perhaps not surprising. For one thing, it has traditionally been very tempting for academics and artworld professionals to propose a level playing field between themselves and the diasporic other. To this end, discussions of alterity, mobility and cosmopolitanism prove much more useful than any discussion of class. Moreover, whenever a group is generally perceived as culturally excluded, rather than working class, this comfortably occludes the question of who really is 'included' in society to begin with, and makes the conflict a remediable one.[4]

To consider Euroamerican ideologies of (post)multi-culturalism without addressing the meritocratic cycle of supply and demand – and thus the currency of the terminology itself – is an uninspiring, predictable exercise. My exhibition project *Ethnic Marketing* – which, at Maria Lind's behest, I presented at the *Fiesta of Tough Choices* seminar – was an attempt to underline how artists travelling from A to B adopt 'culturally specific' styles or discourses as strategies in the wake of brutally uncompromising hegemonic structures. It is becoming ever clearer that the west is not merely an observer of globalised cultural flows but, just like any other demanding client, actively defines the supply.

In the wake of sporadically growing demand, western critics and curators, who are expected to be familiar with vast quantities of work from geographically-removed contexts, are becoming increasingly dependent on a small handful of willing players with a foothold in global centres. A number of artists and intellectuals worldwide are quite comfortable with the idea of using mainstream Euroamerican appetites to their own advantage, but only few are in a position to do so. As some have put it, these exclusive networks are leading to a practice no less arbitrary than the art historical autocracy of the Eurocentric Trained Eye. By contrast, *Ethnic Marketing* allows you to turn the tables and view the Centre of the Real, the Western subject, as part of an 'ethnic' populace, with a specific buying power and demands, to define another type of multiculturalism as a starting point.[5]

In summary, then, it is not so much that the multicultural paradigm is the lesser of all evils, or a pragmatic 'best case scenario'. Rather, it is too facile to consider multiculturalism a sham, on the basis that there are no such concepts that are truly valid, beyond the sense in which 'progress', 'human rights', or even 'zeitgeist' are any more than ideas with prescriptive powers, and not Really Existing stuff we can see, prove, or otherwise authenticate. Terms such as 'roots', 'nation', 'community', 'minority' and 'culture' themselves only barely apply to Really Existing histories on the ground in a descriptive way. And, if the intrinsic dialectics between top-down veracity and grass-roots discourse were not complex enough, the differences between ethnic language and ethnic belonging, between racist language and racism without qualification, make things decidedly more complicated. In addition to this, the conflicting, diasporic stagings of self-identity, most of which have little to do with the identity-political developments in their respective fatherland, are routinely interspersed with intra-cultural differences pertaining to lifestyle, ideology, age and class.

Although part of our initial approach to the *Fiesta of Tough Choices* was a quest for a more sophisticated terminology around these issues, this may lead to a dead end. A century from now, if people are not croaking verbal abuse from their balconies, they will be staging festivals of cultural diversity, hoping for the miracle of multiculturalism to materialise, for Iranian housewives and Tamil taxi drivers to begin discussing art and politics in the foyer of Iaspis. It makes little sense to sidestep the implications of multiculturalism by abandoning them for something more flattering, or by waiting for them to die off; they will not be doing this any time soon.

Notes

1. Tirdad Zolghadr, *Turning Barriers into Sales Opportunities,* interview series on DVD, 2004, c.25 min.

2. Committee terms of reference – Coordination of the Year of Multiculture 2006 TOR 2004:169, Decision at government meeting on 9 December 2004.

3 . Richard Florida, *The Rise of the Creative Class* (Cambridge, MA: Perseus Books, 2002).

4. Beverley Skeggs, *Class, Self, Culture* (London: Routledge, 2004).

5. Tirdad Zolghadr (ED.), *Ethnic Marketing* (Tehran: JRP/Ringier, 2006).

A FIESTA OF TOUGH CHOICES
4–12 MARCH 2006
A FESTIVAL INSPIRED EXHIBITION
WITH TWO SEMINARS

Following the government declaration of the *2006: Year of Cultural Diversity,* Iaspis arranged an exhibition and two seminars in order to critically reassess standard terminologies and beliefs within the debate on multiculturalism. The aim was to examine how the art-world can contribute to this ongoing discussion on ethnicity, politics and culture.

Soundtrack for A Fiesta of Tough Choices, 2006, 1 min loop
Peter Geschwind

Panel discussion with Hito Steyerl, Jonathan Harris, Timothy Brennan, Tirdad Zolghadr, Maria Lind and Måns Wrange.

6.00 PM, 2000
Philippe Parreno and Pierre Huyghe
On the floor a patchwork of wall to
wall carpet represents shadows cast
through an imaginary window.

Jonathan Harris

Feral Trade Catering, 2006
Kate Rich

Loulou Cherinet in the audience.

Interview Series
Video loop, DVD, 6 min
Loulou Cherinet

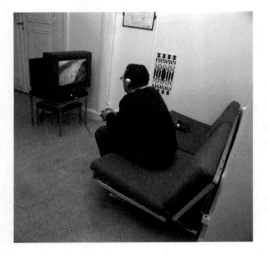

November, 2004, DVD 25 min
Hito Steyerl
The point of departure here is a s-8 feminist martial arts film
which Steyerl once produced with Andrea Wolf, one of her closest
teenage friends. Wolf was later to be considered an enemy of the
German state, and went underground to join the Kurdish guerrilla
PKK. She was shot to death in 1998 in Kurdistan, presumably by
members of the Turkish army. *November* deals with the aesthetics
of political resistance, particularly the gestures, images and iconog-
raphies of radical struggle and protest.

Natascha Sadr Haghighian

Speech Bubbles, 1997
Philippe Parreno
White mylar balloons in the shape of cartoon bubbles,
produced for a trade union. The audience is encouraged to
mark its demand, while still participating in the same image.

Audience playing with *Speech Bubbles*.

A Fiesta of Tough Choices, 2006
Philippe Parreno
Soap in the shape of human hearts.

Timothy Brennan

SELF PRESENTATIONS

Timothy Brennan
Minneapolis

Timothy Brennan teaches in the Department of Cultural Studies and Comparative Literature, and the Department of English, at the University of Minnesota. His essays on literature, cultural politics, and imperialism have appeared in numerous publications, including *The Nation*, the *Times Literary Supplement*, *Critical Inquiry*, and the *London Review of Books*. He is the author of *Myths of the Nation: Salman Rushdie and the Third World; At Home in the World: Cosmopolitanism Now; Alejo Carpentier's Music in Cuba*, and most recently *Wars of Position: The Cultural Politics of Left and Right*. His book *Secular Devotion: Afro-Latin Music and Imperial Jazz* is forthcoming. Brennan has worked as a radio journalist in Central America, a consultant for the Public Broadcasting Service, and a feature news reporter for WKCR-FM (New York) and WBEZ-FM (Chicago). His is now at work on *Borrowed Light*, a study of the colonial obsessions of European artists, philosophers, and social theorists after WWI.

Loulou Cherinet
Stockholm

A documentary and biographical tone pervades the works of Loulou Cherinet. They always include actual people in more or less arranged situations. She makes no secret of the fact that the situations in her films and photos are constructed, but the difference between reality and image is not that great. The actors in her films always play themselves, even if the situation is arranged, but it may not differ much from the situations and the parts they – and the viewer – normally have in the social space. In the video *White Women* (2002), for instance, the setting is a dinner at a large table where the guests, all men of African origin, are filmed with a rotating camera in the centre of the table, as they sit dressed in striped sailor tops discussing their experiences of white women. In *White Women*, as in most of Loulou Cherinet's works, it is significant that the relationship between the depicted people and the viewer feels unsevered. You can never really say that the artist's presence is noticeable in the image, since the depicted appear to ignore the camera, and therefore, the viewer easily slips inside the picture. It feels like getting very close to something the artist wants us to see or hear, but which she does not want to present herself or state out loud. Through these unexpected openings into the pictures, created by documentary dramaturgical means, she opens up the situations that the pictures relate to the viewer. This is an equilibristic play with shifts in perspective and perception both within and outside the picture, two positions that, in Loulou Cherinet's case, always seem to be two sides of the coin. / Rodrigo Mallea Lira. www.cherinet.com

Peter Geschwind
Stockholm

For me, a work can take its point of departure from an idea of error. A misuse of both material and method. Like allowing a certain rhythm or tune to take full control of the form, structure and editing of a video. In my sculptures, I equally emphasize secondary characteristics of various objects and material, disregarding their actual functions, and recombining them in an attempt to generate a glitch or deadlock.

Jonathan Harris
Liverpool

Jonathan Harris is Professor of Art History and Director of the Centre for Architecture and the Visual Arts (CAVA) at the University of Liverpool. He is the author and editor of many books on twentieth century art and society, including *Federal Art and National Culture: The Politics of Identity in New Deal America* (1995), *Art, Money, Parties: New Institutions in the Political Economy of Contemporary Art* (2004), and *Writing Back to Modern Art: After Greenberg, Fried, and Clark* (2005). His new books include *Art History: The Key Concepts* (2006) and the edited collection *Dead History, Live Art?: Subjectivity, Spectacle, and Subversion in Visual Culture since the 1960's* (2007). Harris has lectured around the world on art and politics; on culture, the state, and ideology; on 'new art history', and on modernist criticism in the U.S. in the 1950's and 60's. He chairs the Tate Liverpool/Liverpool University Press series of *Critical Forum* books published since

1992 and is the editor of a new series, *Value: Art: Politics*, also published by Liverpool University Press.

Edda Manga
Cairo / Gothenburg / Uppsala

Edda Manga is a researcher at the Department of History of Ideas at Uppsala University and a member of the network of critical cultural production *Bwana club*. Her area of interest is the relation between western modern thought and colonialism. Currently she studies the *Just War tradition* in western political thought in relation to European colonial expansion. Her latest publications are *Vad är rasism?* (an introduction to race thought in the west) and *Slöjor* (an introduction to the history of the politics of representation of the Moslem veil during the 20th century).

Kate Rich
Melbourne / Bristol

Kate Rich was born in Melbourne and lives in Bristol. As itinerant artist and cultural producer she has been investigating useful models of wagelessness, both for herself and others, which is how she got into the grocery business.

Philippe Parreno
Oran / Paris

In his works Philippe Parreno always searches for ways to provoke a rethinking of the common models for exhibitions, authorship and narration. His interest in non-linear practice and in the whole production process of an artwork or an exhibition is palpable in most of his works. His play with the production of meaning and with narrative structures often involves collaboration with other artists, writers, architects and scientists. The most well known collaboration to date is *No Ghost Just a Shell*, which he initiated together with the artist Pierre Huyghe in 1999. After having bought a Japanese Manga-character – Ann Lee – Pierre Huyghe and Philippe Parreno invited colleagues to give identity to this virtual character in the form of for instance short video animations and other types of works.

Natascha Sadr Haghighian
Berlin

Natascha Sadr Haghighian is part of the *possest* group (www.possest.de). Any part of *possest* group can change. This can include a change of name, coordinates and any other representational data. The *possest* group is working on the dispersion of representational structures in order to confuse the power constellations and value production behind them. Anyone can become part of the *possest* group.

Hito Steyerl
Vienna / Berlin

I work as filmmaker, video artist and author in the area of essayist documentary visual production and cultural criticism. The works are located on the interface between film and fine arts, and between theory and practice, and deal with questions of urbanism, globalisation, and territory. I hold a PHD in philosophy and have taught extensively, recently at Goldsmiths College, London, but also at several other institutions in Berlin, Vienna, Hanover and Munich.

Måns Wrange
Stockholm

Måns Wrange is an artist based in Stockholm, who works with long-term collaborative projects in which he explores strategies that influence opinion forming, such as lobbying, opinion polls and focus groups, as well as techniques on how to alter human behaviour through social organization, objects and architecture. He is the founding member of OMBUD (www.ombud.org), a combination of think tank and creative studio, which conducts these projects and is organized as a network of people from the fields of science, media, politics and the arts. His projects include *The Average Citizen Lobbying Project* (1999–), in which the views of a statistically average citizen affect public opinion through a combination of political lobbying and product-placement; *The Good Rumor Project* (2004–), in which two positive rumours about both sides of the U.S.-Mexican border were created through the use of focus groups, and then spread epidemically through a viral marketing campaign involving thousands of people in Tijuana and San Diego; *The Compromise House* (2001–), an experimental house project where social and aesthetic solutions are based on the principle of compromise as a positive and productive principle. His work is widely exhibited internationally, including shows at Santa Monica Museum of Art, Los Angeles; InSite_05, San Diego/Tijuana; De Appel Foundation, Amsterdam; The Museum of Contemporary Art Chicago; Moderna Museet, Stockholm; Museum of Contemporary Art, Zagreb; ICA, London; South African National Gallery, Cape Town; Shirn Kunsthalle, Frankfurt; Museo Tamayo, Mexico Ciy; Manifesta 4, Frankfurt; Kunsthalle Wien, Vienna and P.S.1 Museum, New York. Wrange is also professor at the Department of Fine Art, founding director of CuratorLab and co-founder of WIRE at Konstfack, University College of Arts, Crafts and Design in Stockholm.

Tirdad Zolghadr
Tehran / Zurich

Tirdad Zolghadr works as a freelance curator, writes for *Frieze Magazine* and has also contributed to *Parkett*, *Bidoun*, *Cabinet*, *Afterall*, *Neue Zürcher Zeitung*, *Straits Times Singapore* and other publications. Since 2004, Zolghadr has curated events at Cubitt London, Iaspis Stockholm, Kunsthalle Geneva, various Tehran artspaces and other venues. He was co-curator of the International Sharjah Biennial 2005, and is currently preparing a long-term exhibition and research project addressing social class in the art world taking place at Gasworks London, Platform Istanbul, Townhouse Cairo and Tensta Konsthall. Zolghadr is also a founding member of the Shahrzad art & design collective and will shortly publish his novel *Softcore* with Telegram Books, London.

Published and distributed by:
Torpedo Press
kontakt@torpedobok.no
www.torpedobok.no
Hausmannsgt. 42
0182 Oslo, Norway

Editors:
Maria Lind and Tirdad Zolghadr

Project manager:
Robert Stasinski

Graphic concept:
Andreas och Fredrika

Copy editor:
Eivind Slettemeås
Line Ulekleiv

Language Editor:
100 % Proof

Printing:
Wassberg + Skotte tryckeri,
Stockholm

ISBN: 978-82-997365-3-4

Contact:
Iaspis
Maria Skolgata 83
118 53 Stockholm, Sweden
rs@iaspis.com
www.iaspis.com

Iaspis is the international program
of the Visual Arts Fund, a branch
of the Arts Grants Committee.

All copyrights between Iaspis,
Torpedo Press, the editors and the
authors. All rights reserved, no
part of this publication may be
reproduced without the permission
of the publisher and the authors.

We would like to thank the
following for translations:
Toshiko Alfaro
Erik Berg
Leya Mira Brander
Alessandra Di Pisa
William Easton
Power Ekroth
Suzi Ersahin
Elisabeth Eurén
Alexander Vaindorf
Ikko Yokoyama

Ⓚ O N S T N Ä R S N Ä M N D E N

Ⓘ A S P I S

TORPEDOPRESS